What Have We Done?

GW00691845

What Have We Done?
The surrender of our democracy to the EU

David G. Green

Civitas: Institute for the Study of Civil Society
London

First Published April 2013

© Civitas 2013
55 Tufton Street
London SW1P 3QL

email: books@civitas.org.uk

ISBN 978-1-906837-51-8

Independence: Civitas: Institute for the Study of
Civil Society is a registered educational charity (No.
1085494) and a company limited by guarantee (No.
04023541). Civitas is financed from a variety of
private sources to avoid over-reliance on any single
or small group of donors.

All publications are independently refereed. All the
Institute's publications seek to further its objective of
promoting the advancement of learning. The views
expressed are those of the authors, not of the
Institute.

Typeset by
Civitas

Printed in Great Britain by
Berforts Group Ltd
Stevenage SG1 2BH

Contents

	Page
Author	vii
Acknowledgements	viii
Preface	ix
Introduction	1
The development of England's constitution	8
An elected king?	9
The emergence of parliament	11
The legal powers of the king and parliament	11
Rule by lawyers	17
Rule by the king alone or the king in parliament	21
Emergence of Cabinet government accountable to parliament	25
The twentieth century: the true political sovereign is the electorate	27
After 1973	31
The choice we face	39
Notes	40

Author

David G. Green is the Director of Civitas. His books include *The New Right: The Counter Revolution in Political, Economic and Social Thought*, Wheatsheaf, 1987; *Reinventing Civil Society*, IEA, 1993; *Community Without Politics: A Market Approach to Welfare Reform*, IEA 1996; *Benefit Dependency: How Welfare Undermines Independence*, IEA, 1999; *We're (Nearly) All Victims Now*, Civitas 2006; *Individualists Who Co-operate*, Civitas 2009 and *Prosperity with Principles: some policies for economic growth*, Civitas, 2011.

He writes occasionally for newspapers, including in recent years pieces in *The Times* and *The Sunday Times*, the *Sunday Telegraph* and the *Daily Telegraph*.

Acknowledgements

I am very grateful to Justin Shaw, Professor Ken Minogue and Professor David Conway for their comments on earlier drafts.

Preface

Since joining the European Economic Community (as it then was) in 1973 we have steadily lost the power to govern ourselves. This pamphlet describes the essential qualities of the free, open and democratic system we have evolved during a thousand years of national life. It goes on to claim that our free system has been weakened but not yet destroyed, and argues that it falls to the generations now living to be more reliable custodians of liberty and democracy, and to restore our heritage before it's too late.

David G. Green

Introduction

We have tended to think of the EU as a useful device for encouraging mutually beneficial trade: no more and no less. When we joined we did not think we were surrendering our national independence. In truth we have been rather naïve in clinging to this view, because all the other members, especially France and Germany, have always made it clear that their intention was to create a European government. That is why France vetoed British efforts to join in the 1960s and it is why at the end of 2012 a Frenchman, Jacques Delors, was among the first to suggest that a way should be found for Britain to have a looser relationship with the EU, perhaps just a free trade agreement.

The claim that the common market was largely an economic co-prosperity zone had some plausibility at the time of the 1975 referendum. It was possible for a nation to veto many decisions that were against the interests of its people. So long as this safeguard remained, the EU might have developed into a mutually beneficial system of international co-operation. But the dominant countries wanted to be able to impose their wishes on other member states. The turning point came with the Single European Act of 1986, which was actively supported by the Thatcher administration. The national veto was replaced by qualified majority voting (QMV) in a dozen key areas, including the single market, monetary co-operation and social policy.

In her book, *Statecraft*, Mrs Thatcher explained that she supported the wider use of majority voting because she wished to force the other EU countries to eliminate 'non-tariff barriers' to trade, which 'operated through different national standards on health and safety, regulations and public procurement policies which discriminated against foreign products, and over-elaborate customs procedures'. She wanted the power to outvote other countries, because she thought Britain would gain at the expense of other EU members, especially in providing services. Without the increase in majority voting, she said, 'the programme itself could not have been driven through in the face of vested interests in member countries whose governments would have been under immense pressure to use the veto'.[1]

Her intention had been to impose de-regulation, but ten years later she admitted that harmful regulation had increased. She acknowledged two mistakes. She had naïvely believed that powers given to the EU to force through the single market would not be used for other purposes. And she had misunderstood the intentions of other leaders. The single market for them was 'a device for centralising more decision-making in the hands of Europe'. In truth, she fell into a trap set by the centralisers.[2]

They knew she wanted the single market and offered her the chance to coerce other EU members, with the intention of using the self-same powers to force the hand of Mrs Thatcher and future British governments. In the end, the Single European Act not only failed to 'complete' the single market—Mrs Thatcher concluded that its powers had been 'abused in order to push corporatist and collectivist legislation upon Britain by the back door'. Her intention had been to impose de-regulation on other countries 'by the back door' but they turned the tables on her. The overall effect had been to 'reduce Britain's ability to compete successfully'.[3]

Because of her mistake, the way was now open for the British people to be coerced into surrendering ever more powers of self-government. What follows is a summary of our constitutional achievements going back a thousand years, showing how much we have lost in consequence of the foolish attempt to twist the arms of other countries, instead of basing international co-operation on mutual respect for national independence.

By the mid-1980s none of the leading political parties attached much weight to the preservation of national independence. The Conservative party, which had once prided itself on its patriotism, had under Thatcher been willing to surrender self-government for the paltry gain of a bigger market share for UK service providers in other EU countries. Thatcher at least admitted her mistake and perhaps her admission may serve as a warning to the current government. It could usefully take into account the alternative view that Thatcher advocated in *Statecraft*. She argued that the strategy of a 'level playing field' was not as attractive as it had sounded. Harmonisation often entrenched unwise regulation. A better approach would have been to allow different nations to compete to discover the best conditions for enterprise. She quotes J.S. Mill, who had argued that Europe owed its success to the 'plurality of paths' followed by different nations.[4]

In saying this she got close to understanding one of the strongest arguments for democratic self-government, one that was stressed constantly by liberal writers including the one most admired by Thatcher, Hayek. Human imperfection was such that we should be wary of giving any agency coercive power. Our institutions should always avoid granting exclusive or monopoly power, and instead should allow for reflection, double-checking, and the correction of mistakes in the light of experience. We should aim for an open society in which different ideas can be tried out, and in which creativity and innovation can flourish. A competitive market allows consumers to compare companies; and in the same way national independence allows comparison between national systems, including their regulatory regimes. Moreover, democracy depends on the existence of nations. They make the ideal of govern-ment by consent a realistic hope and the account-ability of leaders a practical possibility.

Defenders of elite rule have always appealed to what appear to be higher principles to justify their unrestrained power. In an age of religion they claimed that God wanted them to have power. Today, they claim that democracy justifies their rule. EU officials have relinquished a little bit of power to the European Parliament in order to preserve the plausibility of their claim, but in reality EU institutions that look democratic are a disguise for a new mutation of elite rule.

The European Union betrays the unspoken covenant between the government and the people. We give our allegiance to the government of the day and we agree to obey the laws of the land on one fundamental condition: that our rulers act for the common good. But we don't merely take their word for it. Since 1689 we have had the power to remove the government immediately and call an election by the simple expedient of convincing the House of Commons to pass a vote of no confidence. Knowing that an immediate election can be called makes Cabinet ministers behave differently. The right to remove an unworthy government did not emerge unexpectedly in 1689. Before that date we had a tradition of deposing rulers from time to time, with the last occasion in 1688.

The institutions of the European Union are very different. While our system is calculated to make the government take public opinion into account, the institutions of the EU are calculated to isolate decision-makers from public pressure. They dare not make it too obvious that we are ruled by a self-chosen elite and so they go through some forms that resemble democracy. But elections to the European Parliament do not determine where real power lies. The vital element of freedom is lacking: the power to depose the rulers and trigger a general election by a simple majority vote.

What's really at stake is not just the restoration of self-government to the British people, but the survival of British democracy itself. And because we have been taught so little history for the last generation or two, understanding of the crucial elements that make our system work has been very nearly lost—above all, the right instantly to dismiss a government. It has been our tradition for centuries and even applied to monarchs. We don't expect our MPs to be delegates; they are sent to Westminster to learn and to think. Their job is to make laws and supervise the government according to their con-science. Governments unavoidably have a wide discretion, but like all such power it can be abused and frequently has been. Because of this perennial danger, we evolved a system that allowed us to get rid of rulers without the need for bloodshed. It does not guarantee that every government will represent the common good at all times, but it makes it more likely that the views of the electorate will prevail sooner or later. As the great philosopher of the open society, Sir Karl Popper, has argued, it is the single most important condition for the survival of a free and democratic society.[5]

To avoid one potential misunderstanding, a preference for the Westminster system does not imply that a presidential system like America's is not democratic. Their government can be removed without bloodshed once every four years. Moreover, an American president can do little without the support of both houses of Congress. These checks and balances were deliberately installed by the American founders to give the government a strong reason to take public opinion into account. The system lacks the immediacy of the Westminster model, but achieves accountability in a different way. The EU, by contrast, has neither the legitimacy of the Westminster nor the presidential system.

Our system of government by consent emerged from centuries of struggle to retain the advantages of government without allowing rulers to do whatever they pleased. From time to time in our history, kings who misused their powers were overthrown, but after the last such revolution in 1688, the government of the day ceased to be the monarch. Having suffered at the hands of absolutist rulers, the British people resolved that future governments were to be committees drawn from parliament that could rule only so long as they had the support of the House of Commons. A government that lost a vote of no confidence by MPs had to resign and face an immediate general election. It took centuries to evolve this system but since 1973, when we joined the European Economic Community, our ability to remove the real wielders of power has been weakened. Many powers vital to our future are now exercised, not by a government in London that can be forced to face an immediate general election, but in Brussels.

All but a few heroic MPs have remained silent while the power to govern ourselves has been gradually taken from us and given to the rulers of the European Union. But the MPs who actively encouraged this transfer of democratic self-government outside the land had no right to do so. Unless we decide to abandon the centuries-long constitutional conventions described by Dicey (below), we are entitled to view the power of MPs as a temporary capacity to make laws for the British people.[6] They have never had the right to give that power to someone else. While the 1975 Referendum accepted our membership of the common market (EEC), it gave no authority to transfer the right to make future British laws outside the UK. Politicians should have asked permission; and now is the time to restore that power to its rightful owners, the British people.

The development of England's constitution

Our greatest constitutional historians, including F.W. Maitland of Cambridge University and Edward Freeman of Oxford, concur that by the reign of

Edward I (1272-1307) the main features of our constitution were established. The key institutions were the king; an assembly of clergy, lords and commons; a king's council; the high offices of state, such as the chancellor; and the courts of law. Parliaments of the fourteenth century exercised all the powers of more recent parliaments: they dismissed ministers, regulated the royal household, and deposed kings from time to time. But, as the Tudor and Stuart regimes showed, our constitutional traditions were not out of danger until the revolution of 1688 ended the absolutism of monarchs permanently.[7]

An elected king?

The origins of the system lie in Anglo-Saxon times, and the Saxons seem to have been typical of the Germanic tribes described by Tacitus in the first century AD.[8] An assembly elected a king from those of noble descent, and assigned him only limited powers. In England the assembly was the witenagemot, whose membership seems to have varied. It was not a popular assembly but a gathering of 'the wise', including bishops and ealdormen. Before 1066, the assembly had significant power, including the right to elect and depose the king, to legislate along with the king, to give counsel and consent to laws, to nominate bishops and ealdormen jointly with the king, to grant public lands and taxes, and to declare peace and war. It was also a tribunal of last resort for civil and criminal law.[9] Maitland's assessment was that the most admirable element in the Anglo-Saxon constitution was 'that as yet no English king has taken on himself to legislate or to tax without the counsel and consent of a national assembly'.[10]

Before 1066 kings were elected from among the members of noble families, including the last two Anglo-Saxon kings, Edward and Harold. William I based his claim to the throne on his nomination by Edward the Confessor, but the power of a king to name his successor was not recognised by the witenagemot. War followed and William won, but despite taking the Crown by force he subsequently sought the support of the assembly. He was asked to swear an oath to uphold the laws of Edward the Confessor, as did later Norman kings. The death of the Conqueror led to fighting between his sons, Robert and William Rufus, and the approval of the witenagemot was used to legitimise the succession of the younger son, William. These Norman rulers were dictators but they governed with the counsel and consent of the barons, thus preserving something of the Anglo-Saxon tradition.[11] Gradually over many decades, the authoritarianism of the Normans was replaced by a system more fully resembling Anglo-Saxon conventions.

By the time of Edward I (1272-1307) the crown was being treated as hereditary, but before then kings had not been able to rely on hereditary right.

In addition to William Rufus, Henry I, Stephen and John were elected. But Henry III, Edward I, II and III and Richard II followed in correct order. However, Edward II and Richard II were deposed.[12]

The emergence of parliament

The first recorded example of local parliamentary representatives being called to a meeting occurred in 1213, when John summoned four lawful men from each shire to an assembly in Oxford. The membership of the 'national assembly' was identified for the first time two years later in the Magna Carta.[13] Under Henry III (1216-1272) the powers of parliament grew, primarily when demands by Henry for money were met by demands from the assembly for reform. The struggle for supremacy came to a head between 1258 and 1265, when the rebel forces led by Simon de Montfort were defeated at Evesham. Despite that setback, by the end of the thirteenth century a recognisable parliament existed.[14]

The legal powers of the king and parliament

What was the legal status of the king in the thirteenth century? Bracton, a judge for 20 years under Henry III, accepted that the king could not be sued or punished, but was not above the law: 'The king is below no man, but he is below God and the law; law makes the king; the king is bound to obey the law, though if he break it, his punishment must be left to God'. Although the king could not be brought before a court, the common opinion in the thirteenth and fourteenth centuries was that a king who would not rule according to law could be deposed. There was no legal machinery for deposition, as events in 1327 and 1399 show, which in Maitland's view effectively meant that there was 'a right of revolt, a right to make war upon your king'.[15]

The parliament of 1327 felt it had the power to depose an unworthy ruler such as Edward II, but the removal of Richard II in 1399 was of greater constitutional significance. He was explicitly removed for assuming absolute powers not recognised by the English people. Charges of breaking the law were drawn up against him. He had made laws without parliament, and treated private lives and property as if they were at his personal disposal. He was deposed in favour of Henry IV and compelled to sign a deed of abdication.[16]

Richard II had tried to rule as an absolute monarch but his attempt had been rejected. The House of Lancaster ruled from 1399 and is associated with strong parliamentary rule. Sir John Fortescue served the Lancastrians as chief justice and said repeatedly that the king was not an absolute monarch. In one of his most important works, he contrasted England with France, where the ruler was a dictator with unlimited power. Henry V (1413-1422), for example, was a popular king, but when he tried to name his successor, parliament denied him the right to dispose of the kingdom.[17]

A few years later, however, the power of parliament was threatened by the Yorkists during the Wars of the Roses. They asserted the right to rule in defiance of statute. Edward IV seized the throne by force in 1461 and parliament felt compelled to recognise him. Eventually, the Tudors took the throne in 1485 and by 1509, when Henry VII died, the king's powers were clearly defined. He summoned parliament and he could prorogue parliament. He could create peers, nominate bishops, and grant boroughs the right to send representatives to parliament. If elections were disputed, the issue was resolved by the king and his council. These entitlements gave him great influence on the membership of parliament. Moreover, the king's assent was necessary to law; and he could make ordinances. But he could not impose a tax, repeal a statute, or interfere with the ordinary courts of justice. He was bound by law. He could personally do no wrong and could not be sued in a court. But his power was checked by requiring the king to carry out all official tasks through servants who could be sued, dismissed or impeached. The king was the head of the government, but he did not have exclusive control over all executive functions. Parliament took an interest in many details. Some taxes were earmarked, and royal accounts had to be produced and audited. Offices were held during the king's pleasure, but sometimes parliament dictated who his office holders should be.[18]

Despite these limits, during Tudor and Stuart times progress towards government by consent went backwards. Henry VIII frequently used parliament as a mere reflection of his will. It passed bills of attainder whenever he wished and enforced whatever religious beliefs the king preferred. However, it suited Henry VIII to observe the letter of the law. Other foreign kings at the time abolished or ignored parliament but Henry showed formal respect and, despite perverting the law and parliament, his retention of outward forms made it easier to restore free institutions in the seventeenth century.[19]

Tudor and Stuart monarchs argued that parliament owed its authority to the king; while others argued the reverse. Freeman showed that the Glorious Revolution of 1688 restored the true position. For many centuries it had been claimed that parliament was automatically dissolved on the death of the king, and so had no authority without the king. Parliament was indeed summoned by the king's writ, but in the eleventh century kings such as Edward the Confessor and Harold had been elected after their predecessor had died. The assembly was needed most when the crown was vacant and someone had to decide how to fill it. The same was true when the next in line was a child, too young to rule. Parliament had appointed a regent when

Henry III succeeded to the throne at the age of nine, and had appointed a Lord Protector, when Henry VI became king at the age of only nine months. In practice, calling parliament by means of a royal writ was a convenient way of assembling parliament and no more. The right of the people to meet and decide did not depend on the king issuing a summons. According to Freeman, in the eleventh century, 'it was not the king who created the assembly, but the assembly which created the king'.

The truth of his contention was confirmed in 1660, when the Convention Parliament recalled Charles II. Contrary to what some legal theorists claimed, the Long Parliament did not end in 1649 when Charles I was executed. It was recalled in 1660, when it proceeded to choose a king and grant him a revenue. For the sake of form, its decisions were confirmed under a new Convention Parliament, but the work of selecting Charles II had already been done.[20]

The events of 1688 left no doubt about the supremacy of parliament over the king. An irregular assembly of parliamentarians from the reign of Charles II met in December 1688 to depose James II and elect William and Mary. It was claimed that James II had abdicated when he fled the country, but in truth he was forced from office. These events show that it had long been accepted that in times of revolution parliament could be called without a royal writ. By 1688 the doctrine was that parliament should be summoned by writ, but, according to Freeman, 'it was not from that summons, but from the choice of the people, that parliament derives its real being and its inherent powers'.[21]

The irregular meeting of 1688 advised the prospective new king to call a new Convention Parliament, which met in January 1689. It resolved that James II had subverted his contract with the people, and had abdicated leaving the throne vacant. It formally offered the crown to William and Mary. The Convention Parliament was not dissolved until March 1690 and went on to pass the bill of rights.[22]

Freeman's interpretation showed that every act to restrain the arbitrary prerogatives of the crown was a return to the spirit of our earlier law, not only before the Conquest, but as it had developed in the thirteenth century and especially during its Lancastrian heyday in the fifteenth century.[23] No one was king until he had been called forth by the assembly and anointed by the Church.

There are strong counter-arguments. From the Conquest it is true that the idea of hereditary right grew and 'men gradually came to look on kingship as a possession held by a single man for his own profit, rather than as an office bestowed by the people for the common good of the realm'.[24] Moreover, much confusion was caused by Blackstone, who wrongly claimed that kings had not been elected. His mistake was repeated by subsequent authors. But the facts reveal the opposite. As

Edward II, Richard II, Charles I and James II discovered when they tried to act like dictators, an English king received his right to reign from the people. Moreover, when Charles II was invited from exile to serve as King of England, he was trusted with a limited power, to govern by and according to the laws of the land and not otherwise. He, like all his predecessors, was 'responsible to the Commons of England'.[25]

Rule by lawyers

So far we have been concerned about the relative power of the king and parliament, and by 1689 the victory of parliament was complete. But there was another rival for power that came to prominence in the early seventeenth century. Maitland describes the period as a fight between three rivals for final power: the king alone, the king in parliament, and the law as declared by lawyers.[26]

For a brief period, lawyers made a bid for supremacy. They failed, and perhaps their ambitions would not matter much to us if it were not for the fact that human-rights lawyers are using the same ploy to gain supremacy today.

Sir Edward Coke, chief justice for a time under James I, thought that the common law was above statute and above the royal prerogative. Judges, he argued, could hold a statute void on two grounds: first, when they considered it to be against reason or natural (divine) law; or second, if it infringed the

17

royal prerogative. Coke cites precedents but Maitland found them unconvincing. Judges of the middle ages, Maitland showed, did not think they could question statutes in the belief that they were against natural law. It is true that, under James I, judges did claim the right to declare that a statute was not valid law. Bonham's Case of 1610 is the landmark ruling. Dr Bonham was a medical doctor educated at the University of Cambridge who started to practise in London in 1606. The College of Physicians had been chartered by an Act of Parliament and given the sole right to license individuals to practice medicine in London. The College refused to license Dr Bonham and when he continued to practice he was fined £5. He carried on treating patients and the College arrested him, at which point Dr Bonham sued for false imprisonment. Coke, sitting in the Court of Common Pleas, ruled that the Act of Parliament gave the College the right to issue licenses in order to protect its monopoly and not for the benefit of the public. Moreover, when it fined and imprisoned Dr Bonham it was acting as a judge in its own cause, contrary to common law. Coke concluded that, under the authority of the common law, the courts could declare Acts of Parliament void.[27]

When ruling that the College could not act as a judge in its own cause, he said: 'And it appeareth in our Books, that in many cases, the common law doth control Acts of Parliament, and sometimes shall adjudge them to be void: for when an Act of Parliament is against common right and reason, or repugnant, or impossible to be performed, the common law will control it, and adjudge such an Act to be void.'[28]

Judges did not expressly claim the power to legislate, only that the law — common law and natural law — had an existence of its own, independent of the will of any person. The law of nature (sometimes referred to as natural law) and the common law are occasionally treated as if they are the same thing, but in English legal tradition they are very different. The common law is the name for laws enforced by the courts of England, whereas the law of nature was considered to pre-date common law and to represent a higher standard than any human law. It was God's law.

A clear statement is found in one of the most important cases in the seventeenth century, Calvin's case of 1608. It was heard by all the judges of England, including Sir Edward Coke, chief justice of the Court of Common Pleas. It concerned Robert Calvin, a Scot who acquired land in England. Normally an alien could not own land, and his property was seized by Richard and Nicholas Smith. Calvin argued that he was born three years after King James VI of Scotland became King James I of England and consequently was not an alien.

The judges found that the allegiance of the subject was due to the King by the 'law of nature'; that the law of nature was part of the law of England; that the law of nature was 'before any judicial or municipal law'; and that the law of nature was 'immutable' or eternal.[29] Calvin was, therefore, entitled to own the property.

In his 'Reports' Coke describes the law of nature as 'that which God at the time of creation of the nature of man infused into his heart, for his preservation and direction'. This law had been 'written with the finger of God in the heart of man' and the 'people of God' had been governed by it before the law of Moses, which was considered to be the first written law.[30]

The natural 'obedience of the subject to the Sovereign cannot be altered'. Such obedience was due 'many thousand years before any law of man was made'.[31] The laws of nature were 'most perfect and immutable, whereas the condition of human law always runs into the infinite and there is nothing in them which can stand for ever'. Human laws were 'born, live and die'.[32]

Maitland, however, points out that this doctrine had never been a working doctrine. In the four-teenth, fifteenth and sixteenth centuries, for example, parliament had made laws about virtually everything and had not recognised any theory of law above the king or parliament.[33] And the supremacy of common law, divine law or natural law, was not subsequently accepted by parliament. The fount of legitimacy was the king in parliament.

Rule by the king alone or the king in parliament

The seventeenth century fixed sovereignty with the king in parliament and not with the king alone. Moreover, no permanent power by kings to make proclamations had been recognised for long. In 1539 an Act had been passed (the Statute of Proclamations) saying that the king could make proclamations with the advice of his council and that such proclamations had the force of statutes. Breaches could be punished by fine or prison, but not life, limb or forfeiture. The Act was, however, repealed in 1547 under Edward VI, which demonstrated that the king in parliament (not the king alone) was supreme. Powers could be given and they could be taken back. Parliament cannot bind its successors. Tyranny can be undone.

Nevertheless, the Stuart kings maintained that they had a right to issue proclamations. The claimed power was put to the test under James I. In 1610 Coke was asked if a royal proclamation could prevent the building of houses in London and prohibit the making of starch from wheat. He and three other senior judges found that no proclamation could cancel a law or create a new one, but that the king could admonish by proclamation his subjects to obey existing laws.[34]

James I and Charles I ignored this legal advice and used the Court of Star Chamber to enforce their commands, until it was abolished by the Long Parliament in 1641. According to Maitland, Star

Chamber was a court of politicians enforcing a policy, not a court of judges administering law, words that could be applied to the European Court of Justice today.

However, the king had always been permitted to dispense with laws in particular cases. Dispensing was closely connected with pardoning or declining to prosecute a case. The king was said to have been wronged by breaches of law, and if he chose not to prosecute so be it. But this power to dispense with the law in the case of particular individuals is not to be confused with the power claimed by some kings to *suspend* statutes. The bill of rights in 1689 ended suspension totally, but declared only that recent use of the dispensing power had been illegal. The matter had been brought to a head in 1687 by James II's 'declaration of indulgence' that suspended all punitive laws against non-conformists and Catholics. The bill of rights pronounced in unambiguous words that the 'pretended power' of suspension was illegal.[35]

It had long been accepted that the king could not impose a tax without the approval of parliament. However, kings unable to gain parliamentary support for taxation had tried numerous other devices, including forced loans and compulsory gifts from wealthy individuals. The Tudors had raised money by granting monopolies covering vital commodities like salt, leather and coal. They were unpopular because prices tended to rise, and in 1597 the

Commons began to protest. In 1601 Elizabeth had promised not to create more monopolies, but the practice continued under later kings.

Parliament sought to increase its control of all sources of revenue and demanded that kings must seek the approval of parliament, not only to raise taxes but also to raise revenue in other ways. The Petition of Right in 1628 put severe limits on the ability of Charles I to resort to alternative revenues by stipulating that no one could be forced to make a gift or loan, or pay a tax without the agreement of parliament. Charles assented but then ignored the law by ruling from 1629-1640 without calling a parliament. The 'ship money' case of 1634 brought matters to a head. The king ordered coastal and inland towns to pay a tax to cover the cost of ships. The great parliamentarian, John Hampden, refused to pay and the court of Exchequer-Chamber was required to rule. By a vote of 7-5 it found against Hampden. Some of the judges even ruled that the king's proclamations were laws. The king's power, they thought, was absolute. He was wise to consult his people, but it was only a moral obligation. However, when the Long Parliament was finally called, it declared the judgement void in 1641.[36]

Not only did parliament try to control the king's revenue, it also sought to control expenditure. Under Henry IV, parliament had forced the king to render accounts. Under the Tudors the practice stopped, but in 1641 parliament required accounts from Charles I. After the restoration, parliament became even more determined. In 1665 it made money available for the Dutch war, but insisted that it must only be applied to the war and demanded accounts to show where the money had gone. After the revolution of 1688 it was accepted that the Treasury was required to spend only as parliament had agreed. A further important stage in parliamentary control came in 1698 when the civil list, allocating income for the king's personal use, was approved. A primary aim had been to put limits on the ability of the king to bribe MPs with salaries and pensions.[37]

In addition to gaining control of the Crown, the House of Commons also sought to limit the power of the Lords. Increasingly it was felt that the House of Lords should not have an equal say with the Commons on the taxation of the people. Under Charles II, in 1661 and 1671 it was accepted that 'money bills' must be initiated in the Commons and not amended by the Lords. They must take them or leave them.

The independence of judges was also a vital element in avoiding dictatorship. English judges had always held office at 'the king's pleasure' and the majority in parliament wanted judges to hold office 'during good behaviour', so that they were not dependent on the king. However, William III refused to give ground and the issue was not settled until the Act of Settlement was passed. From 1701 judges could be removed on an address of both houses of parliament to the Crown. Judges no longer depended on royal favour but, just as important for their independence, they could not be removed on the whim of the Commons alone.[38]

Emergence of Cabinet government accountable to parliament

The Glorious Revolution set limits to the king's powers. He was below statute, had no power to suspend statutes, could not create a new offence by proclamation, and could not maintain an army without consent. Income could be earmarked for specific purposes, and judges held office on good behaviour, not at the king's pleasure. Special courts were not allowed.

The revolution, said Maitland, was a restoration of the ancient constitution as it stood under the Lancastrians. This meant that, under William and Mary, the king remained a governing king with a policy. William and Mary attended the Cabinet, which was legally a meeting of the privy council. It was only under George I and II that the monarch did not attend, chiefly because neither could speak English.[39]

As in earlier times, the sovereign was still not personally responsible for crimes or misdemeanours, but his agents were. Before 1689 parliament had to impeach ministers, but after that date a vote of censure in the Commons was as effective as impeachment. Moreover, even when ministers were in no danger of prosecution or impeachment, they were no less bound to bow to the will of the House of Commons.[40] The House of Commons had become the ruling power in the nation.

Ministers were in parliament as MPs or lords and had to answer questions. Committees of parliament could ask witnesses to testify on oath and reluctant individuals could be summoned for contempt if they would not attend.

From the reign of William III there was a recognisable ministry that acted with at least some coherence. Previously ministers were individual office holders under the Crown, but under Anne and George I, Cabinet solidarity begins to emerge. There is a single head, a political programme, and a common responsibility to parliament. Under Anne, both Whigs and Tories were in the Cabinet, but Robert Walpole (prime minister from 1721 to 1742) restricted membership to Whigs. Henceforward, ministers represented a party not a king.[41] The king was bound to act on the advice of ministers and had to choose ministers in accordance with the will of the Commons. High offices of state were held at the king's pleasure, but the monarch was required to choose a prime minister who commanded the confidence of the Commons and to appoint his nominees to office.

Officers of state who were not in the ministry, also held office at the king's pleasure but had in fact become permanent civil servants. Normally they were not permitted to sit in the Commons or to play an active part in politics.[42]

The twentieth century: the true political sovereign is the electorate

By the beginning of the twentieth century the main characteristics of our constitution had long been clear. One of the best statements of the longstanding view of the British people is still to be found in the 1915 edition of A.V. Dicey's *The Law of the Constitution*. According to Dicey, the vital distinction in our system was between 'legal' sovereignty and 'political' sovereignty:

> Parliament is, from a merely legal point of view, the absolute sovereign... since every Act of Parliament is binding on every Court... and no rule, whether of morality or of law, which contravenes an Act of Parliament binds any Court throughout the realm. But if Parliament be in the eye of the law a supreme legislature, the essence of representative government is, that the legislature should represent or give effect to the will of the political sovereign, i.e. of the electoral body, or of the nation.[43]

Dicey described how our constitution was made up of both laws and conventions. There was 'the law of the constitution'—the enforceable laws that laid down constitutional principles—and the 'conventions of the constitution'—the habits and traditions that are observed but not directly enforced by law. The conventions had one ultimate object: 'to secure that Parliament, or the Cabinet which is indirectly appointed by Parliament, shall in the long run give effect to the will of that power which in modern England is the true political sovereign of the State— the majority of the electors or… the nation'.[44]

Dicey strongly maintains that 'the electorate is in fact the sovereign of England'. The whole people act through a 'supreme legislature' whose conduct is 'regulated by understandings of which the object is to secure the conformity of Parliament to the will of the nation'. All the conventions that uphold the supremacy of the House of Commons in practice uphold the 'sovereignty of the people'.[45] To prove the point, Dicey examines three conventions: (1) the requirement that the powers of the Crown are exercised through ministers enjoying the confidence of Parliament; (2) the convention that the House of Lords gives way to the Commons; and (3) the right of kings to dissolve parliament against the wishes of the majority of MPs.

The rule that the powers of the Crown must be exercised through ministers who are members of the Commons or the Lords and who 'command the confidence of the House of Commons', in practice, means that the elected part of the legislature appoints the executive. It also means that ministers must ultimately carry out, 'or at any rate not contravene, the wishes of the House of Commons', which in turn means they must reflect the wishes of the electorate as interpreted by MPs.[46]

The same is true of the convention that the House of Lords is expected in every serious political controversy to give way to the will of the House of Commons. At what point should the Lords give way, or should the Crown use its prerogative to create new peers? The guiding principle, said Dicey, is that the Lords must yield or the Crown intervene when it is conclusively shown that 'the House of Commons represents on the matter in dispute the deliberate decision of the nation'. And if the deliberate decision of the electorate is the vital consideration, then conventions guiding the House of Lords and the Crown are rules 'meant to ensure the ultimate supremacy of the true political sovereign', the electorate.[47]

Dicey also shows how the right of the Crown to dissolve parliament affirms the political sovereignty of the people. At first glance this power looks like a continuation of earlier royal absolutism, but as Dicey put it, the reason why the House can in accordance with the constitution be deprived of existence 'is that an occasion has arisen on which there is fair reason to suppose that the opinion of the House is not the opinion of the electors'. In such cases dissolution is in its essence 'an appeal from the legal to the political sovereign'. A dissolution is allowable 'whenever the wishes of the legislature are, or may fairly be presumed to be, different from the wishes of the nation'.[48]

He gives as examples the dissolutions of 1784 and 1834. In December 1783, George III dismissed the government of Charles James Fox and Lord North and installed an administration led by Pitt the Younger. It did not have the support of the Commons and the king dissolved parliament, leading to an election in March 1784. The result vindicated his decision and Pitt's administration was returned. The precedent was established that the Cabinet, when supported by the king (who has the power of dissolution), can 'defy the will of a House of Commons if the House is not supported by the electors'. The fundamental principle was that 'the legal sovereignty of Parliament is subordinate to the political sovereignty of the nation'.[49]

In December 1834 the king replaced Melbourne's Whig administration with one led by Peel. He dissolved parliament, but the election in 1835 went strongly against Peel's administration and the Whigs returned soon afterwards. According to Dicey, the essential point in both 1784 and 1834 was that 'it is the verdict of the political sovereign' or nation that ultimately determines the right of a Cabinet to retain office.[50] The supremacy of the electorate was reaffirmed in 1841, when Peel moved a motion of no confidence against Melbourne. It was carried by only one vote, but an election was required. The majority in the Commons did not think the policy of the ministry was wise or beneficial to the nation and so the government was obliged to resign.[51]

All the conventions of the constitution, according to Dicey, were 'intended to secure the ultimate supremacy of the electorate as the true political sovereign of the State'. Constitutional maxims are 'subordinate and subservient to the fundamental principle of popular sovereignty'.[52]

After 1973

The UK joined the EEC on 1 January 1973, under the terms of the 1972 European Communities Act. Formally the constitution described by Dicey remains in being. The electorate is the 'political sovereign'. But in practice power has slipped away to the institutions of the EU, and now many of our laws are made in Brussels. As we learned the hard way during the long centuries of growing up as a free people, the essence of a democratic system is to be able to dismiss the government of the day and demand an immediate election whenever there is good reason for supposing that the government does not reflect the views of the majority. Public opinion may find its voice in the Commons, which can pass a vote of no confidence; or it can be represented by the Crown, which can dissolve parliament and trigger an election. Dicey's examples of the king dismissing the government are from the nineteenth century or earlier, but the same power has been exercised in modern times. Under the Australian constitution the powers of the monarch are exercised by the governor-general. In the 1970s the government of Gough Whitlam had lost the confidence of the Australian people and was removed by the governor-general so that an election could be held. The governor-general's decision was vindicated by the general election, which returned a new government with a large majority.

This precious ability to trigger an immediate election has not been formally lost, but it matters a lot less when parliament no longer makes all our laws and when much of the executive power lies in Brussels.

There has been a controversy for some time about the proportion of our laws that are made in Brussels. Claims that 80 per cent of laws were made by the EU were repeated for a time. The think tank Open Europe found that figure unconvincing and thought 50 per cent was more likely. However, based on a study of Government impact assessments, Open Europe concluded that 72 per cent of the cost of regulation in the UK was the result of EU decisions.[53]

But, whether the percentage of laws initiated in Brussels is nine per cent (as some EU enthusiasts have claimed) or 80 per cent misses the crucial point. The undisputed truth is that in numerous areas fundamental to the life of a free people, the EU has legal supremacy. In these domains the EU is legally supreme when it wants to be, a fact recognised by our courts.

Under British constitutional conventions a government cannot change the law by signing a treaty. It must incorporate the terms of the treaty in law by an Act of Parliament. The 1957 Treaty of Rome was incorporated into UK law by the European Communities Act of 1972. Section 1 lists the treaties to which it applies and gives the government an extraordinary power to add new treaties to the list by an Order in Council. In effect it can override UK law by using the prerogative power claimed by monarchs but strenuously resisted for hundreds of years except for a brief period under Henry VIII.

Under section 2(1) all laws of the EEC that were directly applicable were immediately enforceable and were to prevail over future Acts of Parliament, if they were inconsistent with them.

Section 2(2) provided a general power to cover European regulations that did not have direct effect but required member states to make legal changes to implement them (such as measures following directives that allowed some room for national interpretation). Section 2(4) provided for future UK legislation. It stipulated that an Act passed after the 1972 Act that contradicted it would not be enforceable by the English courts. It contradicted the longstanding constitutional tradition that it is always open to a future parliament to reverse earlier mistakes or improve earlier legislation.[54]

Where does final power lie in the event of a clash between Acts of Parliament and EU law? Lord Denning commented in 1976 that once a bill 'is passed by Parliament and becomes a statute, that will dispose of all discussion about the Treaty. These courts will then have to abide by the statute without regard to the Treaty at all'.[55]

However, in 1979 he took a very different line: 'In construing our statute, we are entitled to look at the Treaty as an aid to its construction: and even more, not only as an aid but as an overriding force'. If on close investigation our legislation is deficient then, under section 2 of the 1972 Act, 'it is our bounden duty to give priority to Community law'.[56]

Nevertheless, he provided for the possibility that Parliament might decide to reverse the 1972 Act:

> Thus far I have assumed that our Parliament, whenever it passes legislation, intends to fulfil its obligations under the Treaty. If the time should come when our Parliament deliberately passes an Act—with the intention of repudiating the Treaty or any provision of it—or intentionally acting inconsistently with it—and says so in express terms—then I should have thought that it would be the duty of our courts to follow the statute of our Parliament.[57]

The greatest modern authority on the constitution, Sir William Wade, described the supremacy of the European Court of Justice as a constitutional revolution, by which he meant a new 'political fact' declaring where ultimate power was to be found.[58]

He was prompted to make his claim by the final House of Lords decision in the Factortame case in 1990, which concerned the right to fish in British waters. The Merchant Shipping Act of 1894 had permitted foreign vessels to register as if they were British owned, thus permitting them to fish in our waters. By the 1980s some 95 Spanish vessels had registered and the British government was concerned that over-fishing was leading to the depletion of fish stocks. Parliament passed the Merchant Shipping Act in 1988 to require stronger proof of nationality. The 95 Spanish ships could not meet the new tests and a company called Factortame sought an injunction in the British courts ruling that the 1988 Act was contrary to EU law. The case eventually reached the House of Lords and in 1990 Lord Bridge gave the judgement, which found that EU law was superior to the 1988 Act and allowed the Spanish fishermen to continue fishing in British waters. He noted that there had been public criticism that the decision involved a 'novel and dangerous invasion' of the sovereignty of Parliament, but claimed that such comments were based on a misconception:

If the supremacy within the European Community of Community law over the national law of member states was not always inherent in the EEC Treaty (Cmnd. 5179-11) it was certainly well established in the jurisprudence of the European Court of Justice long before the United Kingdom joined the

Community. Thus, whatever the limitation of its sovereignty Parliament accepted when it enacted the European Communities Act 1972 was entirely voluntary. Under the terms of the Act of 1972 it has always been clear that it was the duty of a United Kingdom court, when delivering final judgement, to override any rule of national law found to be in conflict with any directly enforceable rule of Community law.[59]

The supremacy of European over British law is clear enough and it remains to be seen what will happen if Parliament decides to pass an Act that deliberately contradicts European law. But what about parliamentary scrutiny of the executive? The European Commission has far greater powers to ignore parliament than most of our kings. There has been very limited parliamentary scrutiny of European law. In 1972 the government expressed the view that: 'Parliament should be informed about and have an opportunity to consider at the formative stage those Community instruments which, when made by the Council, will be binding in this country'.[60]

In 1974 both Houses set up special committees to scrutinise legislation, the Commons Select Committee on European Scrutiny and the European Union Committee in the Lords. It has long been accepted that they do not provide adequate oversight. In 1978 the Commons Procedure Committee pointed out: 'the ability of the House to influence the legislative decisions of the Communities is inhibited by practical as well as legal and procedural obstacles'. There was inadequate time, national parliaments had no right to be consulted, and there was no control of legislation made by the Commission on its own authority.[61]

Twenty years later in 1998 Parliament stipulated that no minister of the Crown should agree to 'any proposal for European Community legislation': which was (a) still subject to scrutiny (that is, when the European Scrutiny Committee had not completed its examination); or (b) awaiting consideration by the House. However, these requirements could be waived in certain cases, including if there were 'special reasons'. In such cases, the minister was expected to explain the reasons to the European Scrutiny Committee and in some cases the House.[62] A few MPs and peers have become very well informed about European issues, and some campaigners like William Cash MP in the Commons and Lord Pearson and Lord Vinson in the Lords have stood their ground for the British constitution. But the truth is that countless regulations whose future effects can only be guessed at are constantly forced into law after the barest examination.

The EU has power in many areas vital to our freedom. It can force us to implement laws to which our government is opposed, to which the majority in parliament is opposed, and against the will of the majority of the British people. This transfer of power touches a nerve. A decision to consent to laws is a badge of our mutual respect for one another. Choosing to constrain ourselves for the common good acknowledges that the freedom we enjoy is not the 'wild freedom' found in regions of the world where the strong and ruthless dominate the rest, but the 'civil freedom' in which all can share, to the enduring benefit of everyone else. As Locke convincingly showed in the seventeenth century, 'established and promulgated laws' achieve at least three purposes: 'the people may know their duty'; the people are 'safe and secure within the limits of the law'; and the rulers are 'kept within their due bounds'.[63] Rulers that could not easily be removed tended to serve themselves, not the people. If the legislature was always in being, as in absolute monarchies, Locke wrote, there is a danger 'that they will think themselves to have a distinct interest, from the rest of the community; and so will be apt to increase their own riches and power, by taking, what they think fit, from the people'.[64] This is surely how the EU has turned out. EU office holders are no different from earlier rulers who found that they could avoid accountability. They soon realised that they could put their own political desires above those of the common people, and promptly ensured that their own material interests were fully satiated.

The choice we face

We now face a fundamental choice as a people. Do we allow the erosion of our democracy to continue? Or do we take back the responsibility that earlier generations wrenched from the grasp of recalcitrant absolute rulers?

The issue is not the ability of the government to exercise discretionary power as such. Governments have always had a degree of flexibility. But under our constitution the fact that the government can be removed immediately by either the Commons or the Crown changes its behaviour. EU officials have been handed powers by parliament at a time when the constitutional importance of being able to oust the government has been forgotten.

But, while our free system has been weakened, it has not yet been destroyed, and it falls to the generations now living to be more reliable custodians of liberty and democracy, and to restore our heritage before it's too late.

Notes

1   Thatcher, M., *Statecraft*, London: Harper Collins, 2002, p. 372.

2   Booker, C. and North, R., *The Great Deception*, London: Continuum, 2003, pp. 214-216.

3   *Statecraft*, pp. 374-76.

4   *Statecraft*, pp. 376, 421.

5   Popper, K., *All Life is Problem Solving*, London: Routledge, 2002, p. 94.

6   The debate among legal scholars about the transference of legal power to former colonies is not relevant. Here I am speaking of laws for the British people themselves.

7   Freeman, E.A., *The Growth of the English Constitution*, London: Macmillan, 1898, pp. 91, 100; Maitland, F.W., *The Constitutional History of England*, Cambridge: Cambridge University Press, 1908, p. 55.

8   Stubbs, W., *The Constitutional History of England in its Origin and Development* (three vols), Cambridge: Cambridge University Press, vol. 1, pp. 27, 41.

9   Maitland, pp. 55-56, p. 58.

10 Stubbs, vol. 1, pp. 135-36; Maitland, p. 60.

11 Stubbs, vol. 1, pp. 267-68; Maitland, pp. 60-61.

12 Maitland, pp. 97-98.

13 Stubbs, vol. 1, p. 528; Maitland, pp. 64, 68.

14 Stubbs, vol. 2, pp. 90-93; Maitland, pp. 70-72.

15 Maitland, pp. 100-03.

16 Stubbs, vol. 3, p. 13; Maitland, pp. 190-92.

17 Stubbs, vol. 3, pp. 240-46; Maitland, pp. 198, 201.

18 Maitland, pp. 194-96.

19 Freeman, p. 106; Anson, W., *The Law and Custom of the Constitution*, Oxford: Clarendon Press, 1892, part 1, pp. 20-21; Maitland, p. 199.

20 Freeman, pp. 131, 134.

21 Freeman, p. 137, note pp. 217-18.

22 Maitland, p. 284. Freeman, note p. 217.

23 Freeman, p. 155.

24 Freeman, p. 144.

25 Freeman, p. 147, note p. 220; Freeman, 153; note p. 230.

26 Maitland, p. 300.

27 Coke, E., 'Reports' in Sheppard, S. (ed.), *Selected Writing of Sir Edward Coke*, Indianapolis: Liberty Fund, 2003, p. 264.

28 Coke, p. 275.

29 Coke, p. 195.

30 Coke, p. 195.

31 Coke, p. 224.

32 Coke, p. 225.

33 Maitland, pp. 304, 301.

34 Maitland, pp. 253-54, 257-58.

35 Maitland, pp. 263, 303, pp. 305-06.

36 Maitland, pp. 261, 307, 298, 308.

37 Anson, part 1, p. 23; Maitland, pp. 310, 435.

38 Maitland, pp. 310, 313.

39 Anson, part 1, pp. 29-30; Maitland, pp. 388, 395.

40 Freeman, p. 120.

41 Freeman, p. 123; Maitland, pp. 395-96; Anson, pp. 29-30.

42 Maitland, p. 405.

43 Dicey, A.V., *Introduction to the Study of the Law of the Constitution* (1915 edition), Indianapolis: Liberty Fund, 1982.

44 Dicey, p. 285.

45 Dicey, pp. 285-87.

46 Dicey, p. 286.

47 Dicey, p. 287.

48 Dicey, pp. 287-88.

49 Dicey, p. 302.

50 Dicey, p. 288.

51 Freeman, pp. 115-17.

52 Dicey, pp. 290-91.

53 http://openeuropeblog.blogspot.co.uk/2009/04/how-many-of-our-laws-are-made-in.html

54 Bradley, A.W. and Ewing, K.D., *Constitutional and Administrative Law* (14th edition), London: Pearson, 2004, p. 141; Loveland, I., *Constitutional Law, Administrative Law, and Human Rights* (4th edition), Oxford: OUP, 2006, p. 445.

55 Felixstowe, [1976] 2 Ll L Rep 656.

56 Mcarthys, [1979] ICR 785.

57 Mcarthys, [1979] ICR 785, 789; Bradley and Ewing, p. 144.

58 Wade, H.W.R., 'The basis of legal sovereignty', *Cambridge Law Journal*, vol. 13, no. 2 (Nov 1955) pp. 172-97; Wade, H.W.R., 'Sovereignty — revolution or evolution?', *Law Quarterly Review*, 1996, 112 (Oct), 568-575.

59 R *v* Secretary of State for Transport ex parte Factortame Ltd (No. 2), [1991] AC 603. See also Loveland, I., 2006, pp. 480-82.

60 HC Deb., 15 Feb 1972, col 274; Bradley and Ewing, p. 142.

61 Bradley and Ewing, pp. 142-43.

62 Bradley and Ewing, p. 143.

63 Locke, 'The Second Treatise of Government' in Locke, J., *Two Treatises of Government* (edited by Peter Laslett), Cambridge: Cambridge University Press, 1960, para. 137.

64 Locke, 'Second Treatise', para. 138.